Golden
POPPIES
of California

Golden POPPIES of California

In Celebration of our State Flower

Photographer & Author

George D. Lepp

Golden Poppies of California
D E D I C A T I O N

This book is dedicated to all those who have shared the beauty of this flower with me over the years of this project; in particular Warren, Arlie, Tory, Rich, Eileen, Bill, Lanier, Elly, Dave, Larry, Donna and Jeff. Every poppy I see evokes a golden memory.

Published by
Lepp and Associates
P.O. Box 6240, Los Osos, California 93412

Golden Poppies of California
Text and Photography by George D. Lepp

Initial Book Design by Pandora Nash-Karner, Pandora & Company, Los Osos, California
Production Director: Cynthia Milhem, Pandora & Company, Los Osos, California

ISBN: 0-9637313-2-7 (soft)
ISBN: 0-9637313-2-5 (hardbound)
Library of Congress Catalog Number: Pending

Design, digital production and printing by Media27, Santa Barbara, California
Printed in California and bound in the United States of America

The images in this book are available in various sizes as signed artist and special edition prints.
Please visit the California Poppies website www.goldenpoppies.com or contact the publisher for information.

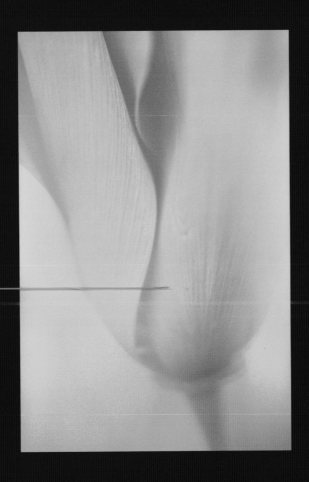

" *There is material enough*

in a single flower for the ornament

of a score of cathedrals. "

— John Ruskin

Table of CONTENTS

Artist's
STATEMENT

The California golden poppy is to me a symbol of each spring's renewal.

For fifteen springtimes, I've awaited the poppies' arrival with restless

anticipation. I have even monitored the rainfalls each winter with

hope of a bountiful bloom. Wet seasons that looked promising brought

excitement, and seasons when rainfall was less than normal brought anxiety.

Even though this project is complete with these pages, I know I will

continue to follow every poppy season, as the golden petals have become

a part of my consciousness. It is my hope that this book will spring a

renewed awareness of the poppy's beauty and compel all to take a closer

look at all of nature. I encourage you to sow the seeds of the poppy's

beauty and help save the golden hills that are its home.

— George D. Lepp

Poppy Reserve

Golden Poppies

INTRODUCTION

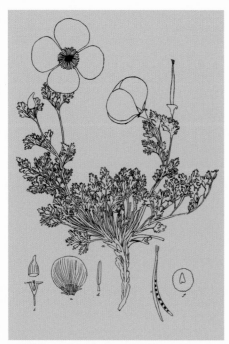

Adelbert von Chamisso's original botanical drawing when he named the poppy.

California's state flower has been a part of the state's history from the earliest explorers who described the brilliant hillsides of color as they came into the area's safe harbors. One description called California *La Tierra del Fuego*, "The Land of Fire," because of the sweeping vistas of poppies along the coast. Later, some of California's Indians believed that the gold miners were searching for the fallen poppy petals. The Spanish had several names for the golden poppies. One such name was *copa de oro*, "cup of gold," another was *la amapola*, "the flame flower," and another is *dormidera*, "the drowsy one," because the flower unfolds late in the morning after closing in the evening or during cloudy weather.

Early sailors referred to the poppy-covered hills in southern California as *La Sabanilla de San Pasqual*, which means "The Altar Cloth of St. Pasqual" in reference to the shepherd in Spain who knelt in the fields of flowers to commune with God. This area is now known as Pasadena, Altadena and Sierra Madre. It is said that ships out at sea could see the fields from 25 miles away. These rivers of golden flowers that ran up the hillsides are long gone. The early padres used poppies on festive occasions to grace the altars and doorways of the missions.

Gorman

"*Out in the rich valleys and upon the sloping hills*

Nature has made her great color show. Here is the home

of the California poppy; the eye can drink from these

myriad yellow cups a brilliant beauty peculiar to

California. Thousands — yes, tens of thousands —

of acres of golden glory enrobe the State in early spring,

a few blossoms lingering like flickering candles till the

season comes again."

— Emory E. Smith
The Golden Poppy, 1902

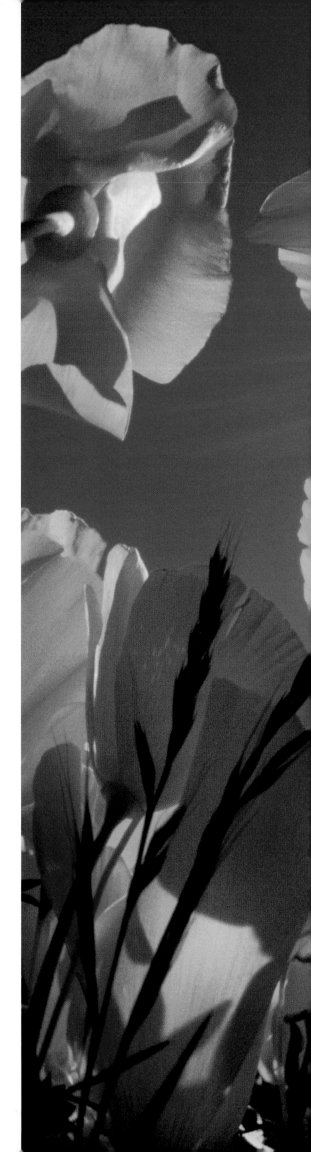

California's golden poppy is
probably the most appropriate
and beautiful state floral emblem
in all these United States.
It has been said that:

"*Its satiny petals, bright with the*
gleam of our gold mines, rich with
the sheen of our fruits, and warm
with the radiance of our sunshine,
typify the ideal of California as no
other flower could."

The golden poppy is revered and sought out each spring by many people and has spawned festivals and celebrations. Due to interest in the flower at the turn of the century, the California poppy showed up as a trademark for many products used daily. Some examples of poppy trademarks were the Golden Poppy Bakery in San Francisco, the Golden Poppy Cleaners and Dryers in Los Angeles, the Golden Poppy Lunch Company in Santa Cruz, the Golden Poppy Ice Cream Company of Santa Clara, and the Golden Poppy Oil and Gas Company of Taft, to name just a few. Even the Santa Fe Railroad used a golden poppy floral design on its serving china. Fruit packing companies in particular liked using the golden poppy on their labels as is shown on this page.

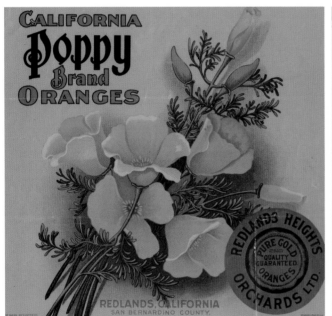

In celebration of the 100 years since the California golden poppy became the state flower in 1903, a school district near the California Poppy Reserve held an essay contest. In her winning entry, sixth grader Liana Meeker describes the beauty of this flower as well as anyone I've heard:

> "*Poppies spread out in front, behind, and in all directions. It looked as if a giant had melted some of the sun and poured it into the fields. Slowly, gently, I crouched down and cupped my hands around a poppy. Its petals felt smooth and soft as silk. This poppy was surely the daughter of beauty itself.*"

— Liana Meeker

Poppy Reserve

San Luis Obispo County

Cuyama Valley

" *My eyes glory across the hills,*

rich in gold poppies and purple lupine hues,

from the very depths of color magic,

I hear history sighing. "

— Anonymous

21

The State

FLOWER

The move to adopt a state flower started at a monthly meeting of the California State Floral Society in San Francisco on September 12, 1890. Three flowers were considered for the honor. They were the golden poppy, the Matilija poppy, and the Mariposa lily. At a December meeting, a closed ballot was taken and the golden poppy won by an overwhelming majority. The only votes for the other contenders were three votes cast for the Mariposa lily.

1890

The press hailed the decision with enthusiasm. The *San Francisco Chronicle* called it, "A most appropriate choice." *The San Francisco Examiner* said, "All the prerequisites of an acceptable floral emblem meet in the *Eschscholzia*." Another paper even said that, "Every man who would show his patriotism for the Golden State must henceforth wear a California poppy in his buttonhole."

Mariposa Lily

Matilija Poppy

The adoption of the state flower still needed the approval of the California State Legislature. As it turned out this was not an easy proposition due to the politics of the time. Mrs. John G. Lemmon, the wife of a noted botanist, and an accomplished botanist herself, headed the movement to have the golden poppy officially named the state flower. In 1895, Bill 707, "An Act to select and adopt the golden poppy as the State Flower of California," passed both the Senate and the Assembly, only to be pocket vetoed by the governor. The only thing to do was to wait two more years for the next governor.

In 1899, the Poppy Bill was again brought before the legislature. Once again the bill passed overwhelmingly and was sent to the governor. The message from Governor Henry Gage was:

"To the Assembly of the State of California I herewith return to your honorable body, without my approval, Assembly Bill No. 229—An Act to select and adopt the golden poppy as the State Flower of California, with my objections thereto. I disapprove of this State selection from the flora of California, because I do not think it a proper subject of legislation."

1899

The Assembly resoundingly
overturned the veto, but the
Senate voted to sustain the
veto, and again the cause was
lost due to political infighting.

Mrs. Lemmon continued the fight and vowed to introduce the bill again and again until a governor was found that would allow it to pass. Four years later, a third attempt was launched in the Senate in 1903. Senate Bill 251 passed the Senate 28 to 1, and the Assembly voted 58 to 1 and then passed it on to Governor George Pardee. This time the Governor signed the bill.

The Senate Journal for March 2, 1903 contains the following passage:

> *Senator Smith, the author of the above Bill, in expressing his gratification upon the same being approved by the Governor, said that Mrs. J. G. Lemmon, who has taken a life-long interest in the golden poppy, and to whose efforts was largely due the adoption of this flower as the floral emblem of the State, was present in the Senate chamber, and he therefore moved that Senator Shortridge present Mrs. Lemmon with the quill pen with which the Governor has approved the Bill.*

The pen was presented to Mrs. Lemmon and the golden poppy was officially designated the State Flower of California.

Eschscholzia californica
CALIFORNIA POPPY

THE WORDING OF SENATE BILL 251:

AN ACT TO SELECT AND ADOPT THE *"Golden Poppy"*

AS THE STATE FLOWER OF CALIFORNIA.

(APPROVED MARCH 2, 1903)

THE PEOPLE OF THE STATE OF CALIFORNIA, REPRESENTED IN THE SENATE AND ASSEMBLY, DO ENACT AS FOLLOWS:

SECTION 1.   THE GOLDEN POPPY (*ESCHSCHOLZIA*) IS HEREBY SELECTED, DESIGNATED, AND ADOPTED AS THE STATE FLOWER OF THE STATE OF CALIFORNIA.

SECTION 2.   THIS ACT SHALL BE IN FORCE AND EFFECT FROM AND AFTER ITS PASSAGE.

1903

Arvin

" *On the wide level acres of the valley the topsoil lay deep and fertile. It required only a rich winter of rain to make it break forth in grass and flowers. The spring flowers in a wet year were unbelievable. The whole valley floor, and the foothills too, would be carpeted with lupines and poppies. Once a woman told me that colored flowers would seem more bright if you added a few white flowers to give the colors definition. Every petal of blue lupine is edged with white, so that a field of lupines is more blue than you can imagine. And mixed with these were splashes of California poppies. These too are of a burning color—not orange, not gold, but if pure gold were liquid and could raise a cream, that golden cream might be like the color of the poppies.* "

— John Steinbeck

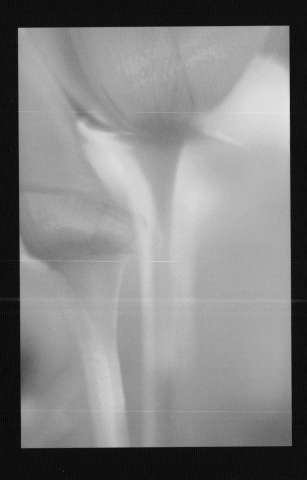

" *Oh California poppy!*

Nature created you as masterpiece,

Simplicity, I can just begin

to understand your wealth. "

— Anonymous

Since 1987, one Californian, David Herndon, has been on a personal crusade to bring back the numbers of California poppies that at one time lined our roadways. His goal is to distribute 100,000 packets of poppy seeds to people all over the state. A number of years ago, Herb Caen, in his popular *San Francisco Chronicle* column, added credibility to David Herndon's project. About the same time, an article in the *Oakland Tribune* called David Herndon "Johnny Poppyseed."

The name has grown with David ever since. The whole idea came to David during his daily commute between his home in Livermore and work in San Francisco where he saw more orange trash bags and fewer golden poppies. If all his packets are planted and nature lends a helping hand, you can expect to see a lot more gold in our state.

David said, "Wildflowers don't need fertilization; sun and a little moisture are about all you need. Each plant produces an abundance of seed pods that can be harvested for broadcasting elsewhere or shared with friends." Herndon also said that the seeds should be broadcast by hand or placed just beneath the surface of the soil, not buried. The seeds should be planted in time to capture the benefits of the fall and winter rains in order to germinate and bloom in the spring. They can be planted in the spring for a later spring or summer bloom. David adds that California poppies have lost their place on rural and country California hillsides because of increased development and roadside spraying to kill weeds.

1987

Poppy Reserve

San Luis Obispo County

"*Nowhere on the continent did Americans find a more diverse nature, a land of more impressive forms and more powerful contrasts, than in California.*"

— Wallace Stegner

Antelope Valley

" *One would fancy that these California days receive more gold from the ground than they give to it. The earth has indeed become a sky; and the two cloudless skies, raying toward each other flower-beams and sunbeams, are fused and congolded into one glowing heaven.* "

— John Muir

Golden Poppies

BOTANICAL

The California golden poppy was first described by Adelbert von Chamisso in 1820, based on a collection of plants made at the Presidio near San Francisco. Chamisso was a naturalist on the Russian ship, *Rurik*, taking part in the Kotzebue Expedition. The ship landed in San Francisco in October, and the California poppies were one of the few plants still in bloom. Chamisso named the plant *Eschscholzia californica* in honor of Johann Friedrich Eschscholtz, his close friend and the ship's physician.

California's golden poppy, *Eschscholzia californica*, can be found from southern Washington down into Baja California, Mexico. Flowers can be seen in Nevada and Arizona, as well. Its distribution is widespread with examples found along the coast, in the deserts, valleys, and most profusely in the foothills of southern California.

Subspecies of *Eschscholzia* are found in the same area, and are partly responsible for the wide range of flower variations. The most common subspecies of *Eschscholzia californica* is *mexicana* (Mexican gold poppy) which is found mainly in eastern California, southern Nevada, Utah, Arizona, and New Mexico. There are some beautiful displays of this flower in Arizona's Picacho Peak State Park, just off Interstate 10 between Phoenix and Tucson.

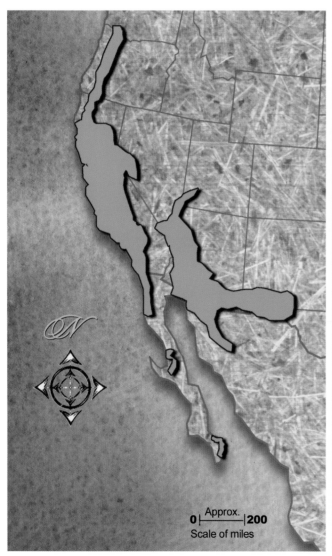

Cayucos

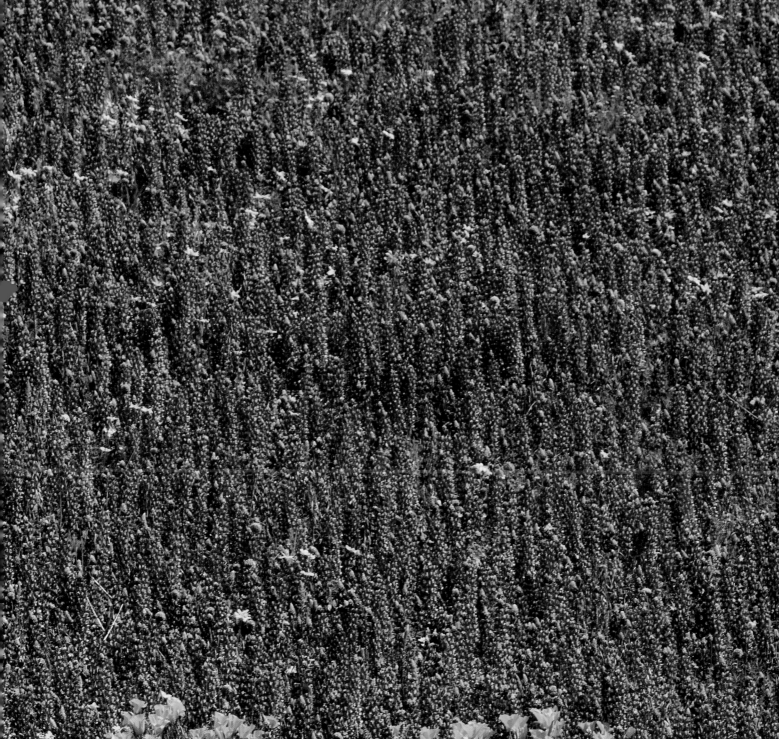

Antelope Valley

The range of elevation for the California poppy is up to around 6,500 feet.

It likes grassy open areas, especially those areas where ground disturbance

has taken place.

San Luis Obispo County

San Luis Obispo County

San Luis Obispo County

After a brush fire removes the choking cover of brush and grasses,

it also affects the ground and seeds to spur a whole new group of

plants the following spring. The flowers that burst forth often

haven't been seen in the area in anyone's memory. In some areas

California golden poppies take advantage of these conditions, and

the contrast between blackened remnants of other plants and a

profusion of golden blossoms is spectacular. Each successive year

the brush returns and reclaims the hillsides, and soon the poppies

disappear with seeds waiting for another chance in the future to

show their colors again.

San Luis Obispo County

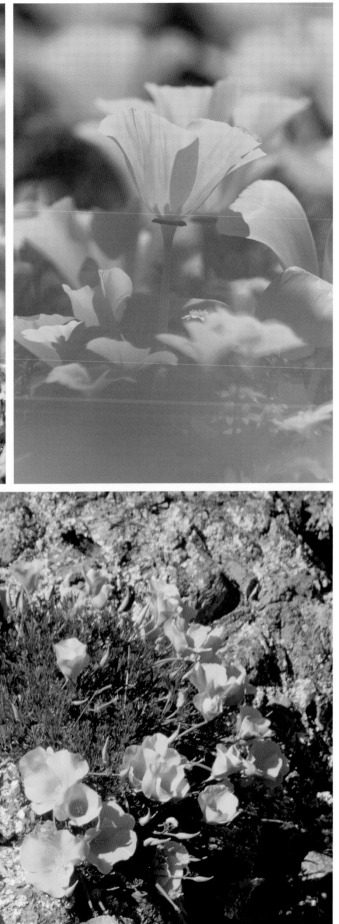

Sleeping Poppies: The early Spanish settlers called the golden poppy *dormidera*, "the drowsy one," because at night and during overcast, windy, and rainy days the flower stays closed with its petals tightly wrapped.

CLASSIFICATION

KINGDOM : Plantae

SUBKINGDOM : Tracheobionta

DIVISION : Magnoliophyta

CLASS : Magnoliopsida

SUBCLASS : Magnoliidae

ORDER : Papaverales

FAMILY : Papaveraceae

GENUS : *Eschscholzia*

SPECIES : *Eschscholzia californica*

Eschscholzia californica can be either a perennial, growing from the previous year's root base, or an annual direct from seed. Those plants with a large tap root can regenerate the following season from the dormant base while others arise from the prolific seed dispersal from previous plants. The slender seed pods can be from 1 inch to 4 inches in length and, when ripe, will burst and disperse the seeds out to nearly three feet.

Near Poppy Reserve

The continuing disappearance of the golden poppy from its native range is due to development, the choking out of the plant by introduced exotic species and grasses that shade out the poppy plants and compete with them for water and nutrients. Also affecting the poppy's abundance are the infrequent burning of hillsides and the compacting of the soil by livestock. The flower does like an area disturbed by farming practices such as disking and will fill in burned areas the next spring with a great show of blossoms.

The botanical history of the California golden poppy includes the use by California's Indians of the poppy plant as a food, oil, and medical remedy. As a food, the young leaves were boiled or roasted, the oil was used in hairdressing, and the root with a narcotic effect was used to sooth toothaches. The resulting mild drug was also used for headaches and insomnia. A group of Indian women in the Palm Springs area was known to use the pollen from poppies as a facial covering or cosmetic.

" *...the golden petals have become a part of my consciousness.* "

— George D. Lepp

Variations
O F C O L O R

The California golden poppy is usually gold to orange in color with numerous variations from white to nearly red. The four petals (sometimes six or even eight) at the end of a long stalk provide a flower that ranges from 1 inch to 2 inches in size. A calyx made of two sepals initially wraps around the flower and covers it like a cap. As the flower develops and the petals open for the first time, this calyx is shed. When this cap separates from the opening flower, it leaves behind a characteristic rim (torus) below the petals, which is a distinguishing feature of the species.

Pollination is carried out by insects, especially beetles. The plant has a gray to bluish-green color, and can vary from a smallish 10 inches to over 24 inches in height depending on location, seasonal conditions, or variety within the species. The leaves are feathery and fern-like from 1 inch to 2.5 inches in length. Examples of the plant can be found every month of the year in some part of the state. The prime growing season is from February through September, with far fewer plants and much smaller flowers in the winter months. The California poppy produces no nectar, so pollinization is carried out mainly by bees and beetles that are attracted by the profusion of fragrant pollen from the many stamens.

"*It is the unceasing effort to compete with the beauty of flowers — and never succeeding.* "

— Marc Chagall

Antelope Valley

A number of reasons are behind the great variance of color in the golden poppies found around the state. Growing conditions and seasonal fluctuations in water and warmth can affect the size of the plants and flowers. The interbreeding of subspecies can also add variety to the plants in an area. Flowers can range from dark orange to light yellow, with spots and shading in some flowers, while others will be of solid color. Some extreme variants can be cream to almost pure white, while some cultivated poppies are crimson red.

"*As they waited for odd jobs*

the Valley burst forth

with one imperial color

poppies flung their gold

over acres of sand

like all the bankers in California

gone raving mad

Women wept in wonder

and hunted fruit jars to can

the precious flowers..."

— Wilma Elizabeth McDaniel

Poppy
NEIGHBORS

"In March and April the bottom of [Twenty-Hill] Hollow [at the eastern edge of the San Joaquin Valley] and every one of its hills are smoothly covered and plushed with yellow and purple flowers, the yellow predominating. They are mostly social Compositae, with a few claytonias, gilias, eschscholzias, white and yellow violets, blue and yellow lilies, dodecatheons, and eriogonums set in a half-floating maze of purple grasses."

— John Muir

Gorman

*L*iving within the brilliant fields of poppies are fauna and other flora. Often we find lupine, owl's clover, cream cups, and gilia in the same fields as the poppies. The end result is a tapestry of color that enhances the texture of the scene. A closer look into the cups of gold finds a profusion of small animals from beetles to tiny bees harvesting the pollen, and caterpillars eating the satin petals. Standing back and absorbing the overall view, we might see ground squirrels, rabbits, coyotes, deer, foxes, and a diverse group of birds living in the open grasslands the poppies prefer.

"*Flowers were born every day,*
and came gushing from the ground
like gayly dressed children from a church."

— John Muir

"*At every stream the road skirted dizzy cliff-edges, dived down into lush growths of forest and ferns, and climbed out along the cliff-edges again. The way was lined with flowers—wild lilac, wild roses, poppies, and lupines.*"

— Jack London

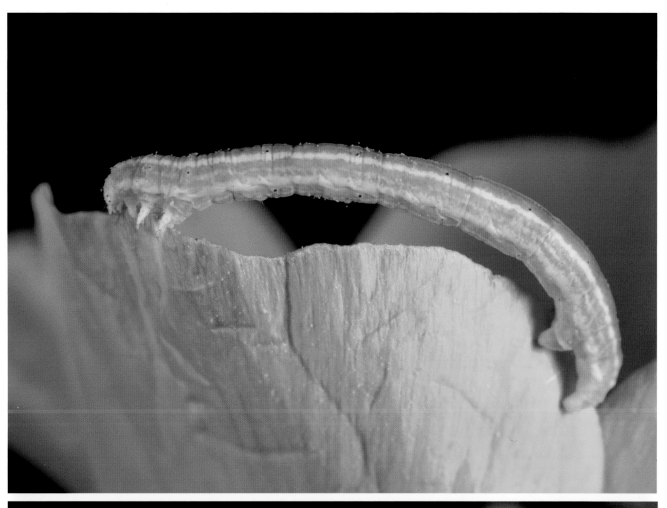

"*People from a planet without flowers would think we must be mad with joy the whole time to have such things about us.*"

— Iris Murdoch

115

Gorman

Where to see
POPPIES

$\mathscr{A}$ntelope Valley California Poppy Reserve—
The effort to secure a place in the Antelope Valley where
the great fields of poppies would be protected was first started
by Jane Pinheiro, a self-taught wildflower artist and botanist.
By the 1950s, she could see the need to preserve the
poppies and Joshua trees in part of a valley that was fast
being developed. Between 1960 and 1964, she persuaded
the state to set aside over 3,000 acres of the valley to
protect Joshua trees, wildlife, and wildflowers.

Starting in 1970, local groups started to raise funds to
purchase the area around Antelope Buttes to create a poppy

reserve. Money to purchase the private land holdings was obtained through the collections of pennies by area schools and the selling of "deeds" to preserve a small part of the land. A "deed" donation of $650 "bought" an acre, $5 "bought" 300 square feet of preservation. In total, 1,745 acres were secured and, on April 24, 1976, the land was turned over to the state and dedicated as the Antelope Valley California Poppy Reserve.

The Visitor Center built on the site, opened in 1982, was named after Jane Pinheiro. The Visitor Center is staffed by the Poppy Reserve/Mojave Desert Interpretive Association (PR/MDIA) which supports the educational projects and programs for school children and the visiting public at several state parks in the Antelope Valley area.

The California Poppy Reserve (located 15 miles west of Lancaster) usually opens in mid-March and has seven miles of trails that include paved sections for wheelchair access. The elevation of the Reserve is from 2,600 to 3,000 feet and is considered high desert. Only day-use is permitted (hiking and picnicking). The number of flowers varies greatly from year to year depending on the moisture, timing of the moisture, and warmth during the winter and spring months. The California State Parks System doesn't water any of the area to stimulate the plants into blooming. However, in order to foster a more natural and increased bloom, the park has used prescribed burning since 1994 to reduce ground litter and decrease the exotic species that compete with the poppies.

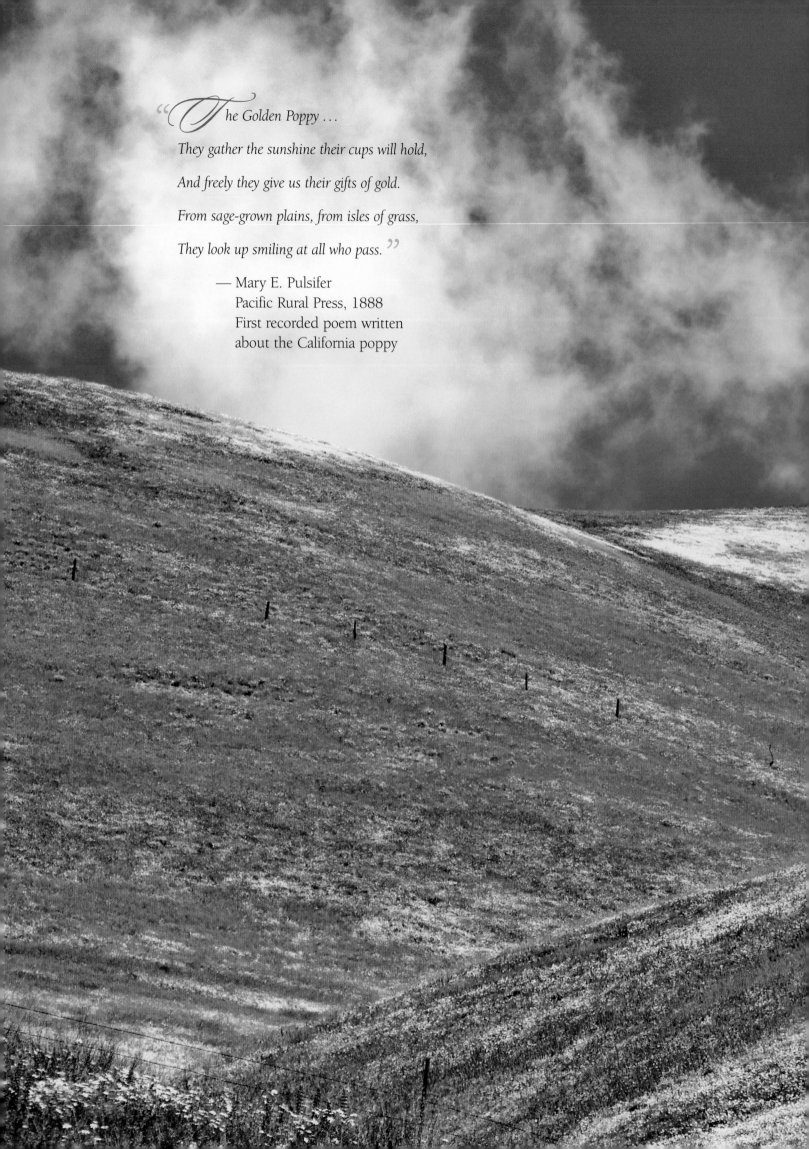

"The Golden Poppy . . .

They gather the sunshine their cups will hold,

And freely they give us their gifts of gold.

From sage-grown plains, from isles of grass,

They look up smiling at all who pass."

— Mary E. Pulsifer
  Pacific Rural Press, 1888
  First recorded poem written
  about the California poppy

Gorman

Poppy Reserve

Ripley Desert Woodland

POPPY RESERVE

Lancaster Road

Munz Ranch Rd.

170th St. West

110th St. West

(Hwy. 138)

West Avenue F

West Avenue G

West Avenue I

60th St. West

Antelope Valley Fwy. (Hwy 14)

Rosamond

East Avenue F

Lancaster

East Avenue G

East Avenue H

East Avenue I

Palmdale

N

Map to California Poppy Reserve

Southern California—The premier area to see expanses of poppies is Antelope Valley, north of Los Angeles and close to the town of Lancaster. Highway 138 runs through the Valley and past the California Poppy Reserve. As you follow Highway 138 east from Highway 14, you will see numerous large fields of poppies glowing on the southern slopes of hills of the Tehachapi Mountain Range. A number of dirt roads will take you up into these fields. Be aware that most fenced areas are part of the Tejon Ranch and are private property.

Where Highway 138 ends at Interstate 5, continue north and watch for the small town (off-ramp) of Gorman. The road that parallels Interstate 5 allows access to some very beautiful wildflower fields.

There are some large displays in a wet year in the Perris Reservoir area. The best way to find out the status and location of a particular year's wildflower bloom is to check a website called www.calphoto.com. This site covers the whole state and will pinpoint many areas that might have excellent poppy displays.

Antelope Valley

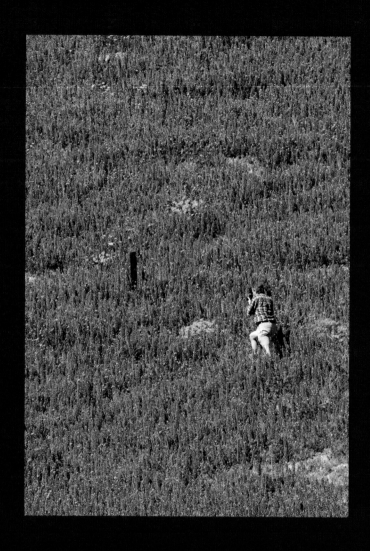

"*When the rush for gold first began in California,*

the Indians are said to have expressed the belief

that the petals of the 'Great Spirit Flower'

(the Golden Poppy), dropped year after year, sank

into the earth and gradually formed the bright

metal for which the strangers were searching."

—Emory E. Smith
The Golden Poppy, 1902

"*When California was wild, it was one sweet bee-garden throughout the entire length, north and south, and all the way across from the snowy Sierra to the ocean. ... The Great Central Plain of California, during the months of March, April, and May, was one smooth, continuous bed of honey-bloom, so marvelously rich that, in walking from one end of it to the other, a distance of more than 400 miles, your foot would press about a hundred flowers at every step.*"

— John Muir

" *Before studying the flowers of this valley and their sky, and all of the furniture and sounds and adornments of their home, one can scarce believe that their vast assemblies are permanent; but rather that, actuated by some plant purpose, they had convened from every plain and mountain and meadow of their kingdom, and that the different coloring of patches, acres, and miles marks the bounds of the various tribes and family encampments.* "

— John Muir

Antelope Valley

Nestled between Bakersfield and the southern end of the
San Joaquin Valley is the small farm community of Arvin.
Running through this town is Route 223, which winds
east through the hills to Highway 58. As the road twists
into the Tehachapi foothills there can be—on a good
flower year—great vistas of flowers that overlook the
valley. Much of this land is privately owned so be
careful to avoid trespassing.

Shell Creek, San Luis Obispo County

Shell Creek—From San Luis Obispo take Highway 101 north to the Santa Margarita off-ramp (9 miles). This is the start of Highway 58. Follow Highway 58 through town and watch for the right turn at the end of the business district. Continue on Highway 58 for approximately 19 miles to the intersection of Shell Creek Road and Highway 58. Many fields of flowers will be evident in the area and for a mile or so up Shell Creek Road. The best time for flowers is the last week in March through the second week of April.

Northern California—Poppies can be found sporadically in many areas
of northern California. Specific areas for the best wildflower blooms are
Bear Valley along Highway 20 between Williams and Clear Lake, and
Mount Diablo near Walnut Creek. The areas along Highway 49 that skirt
the eastern flank of the San Joaquin Valley have displays of California golden
poppies in early spring, depending on that season's weather conditions.

Poppy

Along the hillside

she emerges

   in the light of day

a tender beauty

   soft

     fragrant

she opens her wings

to the sun above

   sensuous

     and confident

she smiles at the turquoise sky

and performs

a ballet of her choosing

   in the warm breeze

she whispers

   to her companions

together

they fill the air

   with brilliant color

   and spring song …

— Daryl Kessler

Growing your
OWN POPPIES

The seeds can be sown in the fall as the first rains start, while in colder climates it will be best to wait and plant in early spring. The soil is best disturbed with rake or rototiller. The seeds can then be sown on the surface and gently rolled or raked into the soil. You do not want to bury the seeds deep. The soil needs to have good drainage. Pick an area with sunny conditions and expect some rain or watering during the growing season to produce the best plants. When the plants start to sprout, do not try to transplant them. Poppies do not transplant well, nor do they grow well in small containers. In subsequent seasons, the poppies will come up on their own from seed dispersal and in some cases will regenerate from the base of mature plants.

Some people believe that the state flower has special protection and can not be picked, even in their own gardens. In reality, you can pick all the poppies you want on private property. With any removal of plants from public lands, you would need a permit from the governmental agency in charge of that area.

" *Of all the wonderful things in the wonderful universe of God, nothing seems to me more surprising than the planting of a seed in the blank earth and the result thereof. Take that Poppy seed, for instance: it lies in your palm, the merest atom of matter, hardly visible, a speck, a pin's point in bulk, but within it is imprisoned a spirit of beauty ineffable, which will break its bonds and emerge from the dark ground and blossom in a splendor so dazzling as to baffle all powers of description.* "

— Celia Thaxter

California's Cup Of Gold

" *The Golden Poppy is God's gold;*

The gold that lifts, nor weighs us down,

The gold that knows no miser's hold

The gold that banks not in the town,

But careless, laughing, freely spills

Its hoard far up the happy hills —

Far up, far down, at every turn —

What beggar hath not gold to burn? "

— Joaquin Miller

There are numerous companies providing poppy seeds in several varieties. Growing California poppies is as rewarding as it is beautiful. Enjoy!

California Poppies

God placed his hand upon the earth

And blessed the sand below.

Then out of the desert's barren ground,

We watch as sunshine grows

A bloom of vibrant orange

Blankets the hills that we call home.

Carefully seeded through tender winds,

A legacy of treasure sown.

— Wendy L. Kohlhoff

"Poppy petals fall

Softly, quietly,

Calmly.

When they are ready."

—Etsujin

George D. Lepp

PHOTOGRAPHER
& AUTHOR

George Lepp has had a lifelong passion for nature photography, and he is one of today's foremost nationally-recognized nature photographers.

His daily schedule routinely includes eighteen-hour workdays, with him smiling all the way. He has achieved what many search for: love of his work. His photography blends his artistic perspective, knowledge of biology, and cutting-edge technical expertise. He is sought after by major photographic equipment manufacturers and publishers of leading photography magazines. In a very competitive field, his professional opinion is highly respected.

His love of nature led him to the training which would prepare him for his chosen profession. College work in the natural sciences prepared him with background information on his subjects. Service in the U.S. Marine Corps as a graphic artist helped to develop his visual acuity and artistic flair. He credits both of these areas of training as a foundation for success in the field. He honed these skills and received his formal training in photography at the Brooks Institute of Photography in Santa Barbara, California, from which he graduated in 1972. He has been a working professional photographer ever since.

Today he travels around the nation giving seminars on nature/outdoor photography and digital photography to avid hobbyists and aspiring professionals. He is frequently called upon to lecture nationally and internationally, and has the endorsement of major players such as Canon, Kodak, and Epson. His stock photography is represented worldwide by Getty, Corbis, Photo Researchers, and AgStock. He has given workshops and acted as resource person in photo shoots in Alaska, Antarctica, Olympic National Park, Galapagos, Yellowstone National Park, and Churchill, Manitoba, Canada (polar bears). He has won numerous national and international awards. His work has been exhibited in museums as well as in the corporate offices of Kodak, Canon and Epson.

In addition to his programs, George is the author of several books, including two successful books on photographic techniques which he both authored and published: *Beyond the Basics* and *Beyond the Basics II*. He is Field Editor for both *Outdoor Photographer* (see his popular column "Tech Tips") and *PC Photo* magazines, and writes regular columns for both magazines. He has a large following of faithful subscribers to his quarterly journals, *The Natural Image* and *The Digital Image*, for which he writes articles on a wide array of topics of interest to the nature photographer. He is never one to keep trade secrets and encourages photographers of all levels of expertise.

PHOTOGRAPHING CALIFORNIA'S GOLDEN POPPIES

My love affair with the golden poppy began a little over 15 years ago when a friend's van broke down not far from Antelope Valley. I volunteered to take him back to pick up his repaired vehicle and at the same time spend the day photographing the poppies for the first time. I wasn't prepared for the sight of endless acres of brilliant orange. That photographic session started an annual trek to find the best poppies each spring.

My poppy project started just after I had switched to Canon cameras, so every image in this book has been taken with their equipment. The progression of camera bodies sounds like the development of the Canon system starting with the T90 SLR camera and soon moving on to the EOS system. The first EOS used was the 630, then the EOS-1, EOS-1n, EOS-3, and my last film camera, the EOS-1v. For the last two years my photography has completely switched to digital and some of the images published here were taken with the Canon EOS-D60, 10D, and most recently the EOS-1Ds.

The lenses used to take the images here have remained pretty much the same from the beginning to today's digital bodies. Even though the media might have changed, the techniques haven't. The staple lenses for flowers are macro lenses, and I employed all that Canon had to offer. The 50mm, 100mm, and 180mm macro lenses were used often. During the last two years, I've used the new MP-65mm 1x-5x macro lens to take the extreme close-ups of insects and flower parts. A favorite technique I apply to flower photography is the use of a telephoto lens set to a large aperture like f/4 to minimize my depth of field and completely throw the background out of focus. To accomplish this, I attach a 75-300mm or 100-400mm zoom lens and an extension tube to my camera for closer focus. When taking overall landscapes I used wide-angle lenses, of which my favorite is the EF 17-35mm f/2.8L zoom. A few images in the book were taken with the 15mm fisheye lens.

Flash was used on some of the close-up images. I often prefer to use flash in conjunction with ambient light to maintain a natural look.

A polarizer filter was occasionally attached to the lenses to darken the sky, and a graduated neutral density filter to maintain color in a bright sky while keeping detail in the darker foreground.

George Lepp and Warren Karber on the first day of the 15-year photographic poppy odyssey.

© *Richard Hansen*

The type of film used in this project changed as time went on. Originally, it was Kodachrome 64, then Ektachrome E100SW, and finally E100VS. In the past two seasons, film was replaced by digital capture and the optimizing of files in the computer. I can assure you that you will not be able to tell which images in this book were captured on film and which were taken with a digital camera.

Part of the reason for the consistency of color over the 15 years of different films and digital capture is that I have taken all of the images you see here and optimized them in a computer using Adobe Photoshop. I use the word optimize instead of "manipulate" because the only changes to these images have been to improve color and contrast to match what I remembered from being there. Occasionally, I will remove a white rock or other obtrusive element to clarify the original image.

The panoramas in this book are comprised of a number of images that were assembled in Adobe Photoshop to make a single longer image. They may be made up of anywhere from two to a dozen images.

I have always considered my camera as a window into the natural world and a way to show non-photographers the beauty that exists before us. If you're a photographer, the camera will help you to see more and look closer. If you're not a photographer, I hope these images will give you new appreciation for the beautiful State Flower of California and nature in general.

ACKNOWLEDGEMENTS

When a photographic project takes 15 years to complete, many individuals get involved along the way. Over the years, people have called to advise me of excellent poppy blooms in out-of-the-way places. Carol Leigh's website has been especially helpful in keeping track of each year's bloom, and anyone can benefit from her service at www.calphoto.com.

One of the best places to see California poppies is the Tejon Ranch in the Antelope Valley west of Lancaster. During the height of the poppy season for several years, a Tejon ranch worker named George opened sections of the ranch to the public for a fee. Without this access, a number of the best images in this book wouldn't have been possible.

The text in this book isn't extensive, but the information needed to be factual. Some of those facts had to be unearthed from the depths of the California State Archives, the reference desk of the San Luis Obispo City-County Library, and the Los Osos County Library. At every turn we had great cooperation and enthusiasm to find the information we were looking for. Additional research on quotes was accomplished by Charlyn Hinz and Shirley Nash.

As the poppy book project progressed from a file cabinet and hard drive filled with images to a collection that resembled a potential book, additional creative people became involved. Designer Pandora Nash-Karner and production director Cynthia Milhem started the assembly and provided the creative direction so important to the project. Media 27 in Santa Barbara, California, then took the handoff and tuned the design and mechanicals to finish the book-making process. The creative team of Mike Verbois, Shukri Farhad, and Phuong Huynh, made it materialize on paper.

There are always those who aren't directly involved in the photography and design, yet whose involvement helps to improve the quality of the final result. My staff at Lepp and Associates helped immeasurably. Tim Grey's editing and input was critical. Julie Corpuel's sharp editing eye was invaluable. Eileen Karber kept the images organized and offered office support. Her late husband, Warren, was there with me photographing poppies at the very onset of the project.

It's always helpful to have the best tools available. Between Canon, Kodak, and Epson I knew that the limiting factor was always me and not the cameras, lenses, films and printers. Dave Metz at Canon has helped at every turn through the evolution of cameras from film through digital. Many people at Kodak helped with excellent color films until digital capture changed my direction. Dan "Dano" Steinhardt at Epson (who also originally helped the project while at Kodak) has supplied me with incredible inkjet printers to proof the book and produce prints to match the beauty of the subject.

Finally—and most importantly—my wife Arlie has coordinated the project and offered encouragement and "life support" to make the book happen. She shines in these pages just like all the other beautiful golden blossoms.

CALIFORNIA STATE ARCHIVES

ATTRIBUTIONS

Page 5: John Ruskin. Reprinted from *Stones of Venice* by John Ruskin, 1851; Page 13: Emory E Smith. Reprinted from *The Golden Poppy*, 1902; Page 14: Anonymous; Page 18: Liana Meeker. California Centennial Celebration Essay Contest Winner sponsored by PR/MDIA, 2003. Reprinted by permission of author; Page 21: Anonymous. Reprinted with permission of author who wishes to remain anonymous; Page 26: Governor Henry Gage. Reprinted from a message to the U.S. Legislature in 1899; Page 33: From *East of Eden* by John Steinbeck, copyright 1952 by John Steinbeck, renewed (c) 1980 by Elaine Steinbeck, John Steinbeck IV and Thom Steinbeck. Used by permission of Viking Penguin, a division of Penguin Group (USA) Inc.; Page 37: Anonymous. Reprinted with permission of author who wishes to remain anonymous; Page 41: Wallace Stegner. Reprinted from forward by Wallace Stegner to *The Wilder Shore* by Morley Baer and David Rains Wallace, 1984 by permission of Mary Stegner; Page 43: John Muir. Reprinted from *Steep Trails* by John Muir, 1918; Page 74: Marc Chagall. Reprinted from *My Life* by Marc Chagall, 1985 by permission of Artists Rights Society (ARS), New York/ADAGP, Paris; Page 83: Wilma Elizabeth McDaniel. Reprinted from *First Spring in California 1936* by Wilma Elizabeth McDaniel, by permission of author; Page 86: John Muir. Reprinted from *A Thousand-Mile Walk to the Gulf* by John Muir, 1916; Page 99: John Muir. Reprinted from *A Thousand-Mile Walk to the Gulf* by John Muir, 1916; Page 106: Jack London. Reprinted from *Four Horses and a Sailor* by Jack London, 1917; Page 112: From *a Fairly Honourable Defeat* by Iris Murdoch, copyright (c) 1970 Irene Alice Murdoch. Used by permission of Viking Penguin, a division of Penguin Group (USA) Inc.; Page 122: Mary E. Pulsifer. Reprinted from *The Golden Poppy*, 1902; Page 126: Emory E Smith. Reprinted from *The Golden Poppy*, 1902; Page 128: John Muir. Reprinted from The Mountains of California by John Muir, 1894; Page 129: John Muir. Reprinted from *A Thousand-Mile Walk to the Gulf* by John Muir, 1916; Page 135: Daryl Kessler. Reprinted from a poem by Daryl Kessler, 1996 by permission of author; Page 139: Celia Thaxter. Reprinted from *From An Island Garden* by Celia Thaxter, 1894; Page 140: Joaquin Miller. California's Cup of Gold/God's Gold. Reprinted from *The Golden Poppy*, 1902; Page 142: Wendy L. Kohlhoff. Reprinted from *California Poppies* by Wendy L. Kohlhoff, 1998 by permission of author; Page 144: Etsujin. Reprinted from a haiku by Etsujin (1656-1739).